FROM THIS
HIGH PLACE

FROM THIS HIGH PLACE

HIGH PLACE

Reflections on Living a Life
of Courage and Purpose

Ken Standley

A Perigee Book

A Perigee Book
Published by The Berkley Publishing Group
200 Madison Avenue
New York, NY 10016

This is a revised edition of a book previously published under
the title *Your Death Is None of Your Business: Your Business Is
Your Life and What You're Going to Do with the Rest of It*,
copyright © 1995 by Ken Standley.

Mywã edition published 1995
First Perigee edition: January 1997

Published simultaneously in Canada.

The Putnam Berkley World Wide Web site address is
http://www.berkley.com/berkley

Library of Congress Cataloging-in-Publication Data

Standley, Ken.
    [Your death is none of your business]
    From this high place : reflections on living a life of
courage and purpose /
Ken Standley. — 1st Perigee ed.
        p.   cm.
    Previously published under title : Your death is none of
your business. Fresno, Calif. : Mywã Pub., 1995.
    ISBN 0-399-52286-7
    1. Death—Religious aspects.   2. Terminally ill—
Religious life.   3. Spiritual life.   4. Standley, Ken.   I. Title.
BL504.S72   1996
291.4'4—dc20   96-22916
                                                CIP

Printed in the United States of America

10   9   8   7   6   5   4   3   2   1

Dedicated to Emma, my wonderful wife, valued partner, trusted advisor and best fishin' buddy, whose pain and endurance are greater than mine

Special thanks and enduring gratitude to Ulmon and Betty Bray, two of the most beautiful people I have ever met, and to Lora Mitrovich, whose steadfast and true support created a precious legacy of her love.

Contents

FROM THIS
HIGH PLACE

Press On, Gallant Pilgrim

gal-lant: adj. spirited, brave

pil-grim: n. one who journeys for a purpose

In May of 1995, my wife and I marked the date of my fifty-eighth birthday with a quiet dinner together. Later, in the cool of the evening, I sat alone on our patio stroking the back of my pushy old cat, Sediki. The question occupying my mind: Is this the year of my death?

This is perhaps a strange question for someone who is only fifty-eight years old, but I had, and still have, strong reasons for believing my death may occur within the next few months.

The threat of terminal illness is no stranger to me. When I was only eighteen, I confronted my first health crisis with the diagnosis of fibrous sarcoma, a particularly deadly form of cancer. I vividly recall sitting in Dr. Willoughby's office. Acrid smoke from his ever-present pipe filled the room.

"How old are you, son?" he had asked.

"Eighteen years old, sir," I replied. I was nervous and clearly anxious.

"Hmm," Dr. Willoughby mused. "Your age will work to your advantage. If we should have to take the arm off, you're young enough to learn to make do without it. You'll be fine."

Following the diagnosis, there had been two surgical attempts to excise the malignancy. But, with the third occurrence of the insidious disease, the doctor and I were discussing the possibilities of some extremely drastic measures.

Fortunately, I did not lose my arm and I survived my first bout with cancer. At the time fewer than five percent of those who contracted this malignancy were as fortunate.

But there were many more health crises to come. They included heart attacks, two open-heart surgeries, removal of the small but vitally important thyroid gland, kidney failure, arthritis, joint replacement, prostate disease, more malignancies, and most recently the prospect of a third open-heart surgery. There were so many life-threatening episodes that one of my doctors unwittingly remarked, "It almost seems like your body is trying to kill you, Ken." His words proved ominously prophetic.

My body is, indeed, trying to kill me.

This startling fact was disclosed to me in 1992,

when a DNA profile revealed that I have an extremely high plasma level of the LP(a) gene. This news was devastating for my family and me. A high plasma level of the LP(a) gene is a valid predictor of premature death.

Medical researchers describe the LP(a) gene by saying that this gene, like other genes, is a DNA code. These codes are much like computer chips that program computers to do certain things in given situations. DNA codes program the body to develop certain traits and characteristics and also to do certain things in given situations. My own exhaustive research into medical studies on the subject revealed that high plasma levels of the LP(a) gene program the body to die, often of cardiovascular disease, by age fifty-eight.

This was the reason for my quiet introspection on the patio following my birthday dinner.

The unusually high plasma level of the LP(a) gene in my gene pool seems to explain my bizarre medical history. Evidently, my body, obeying the dictates of the gene, is doing everything possible to assure an early exit from life and indeed has made several serious attempts to do so. It will undoubtedly relentlessly continue the attack until it succeeds in fulfilling the programming dictates of the LP(a) gene.

As strange as it may seem, I have not experienced fear, despair, hopelessness or even much anger as a result of the discovery of this insidious little gene. This is not because I am in denial, or brave, or even particularly well-adjusted. The fact is, I believe my death is none of my business. I firmly believe my business is my life and what I'm going to do with the rest of it.

Instead of worrying about my death, I use my

health difficulties to help sharpen my awareness of my life as a precious gift. By carefully directing my focus and energy, my threatening health problems provide me with a stimulating sense of urgency and even enthusiasm.

Like John Muir, the venerable naturalist of the High Sierra who would climb to the top of the tallest trees during raging storms so he could feel the power and majesty of the storm, I believe my diabolical little gene has helped me climb to a high spiritual place where I can experience the power and majesty of life.

From this high place I see many wondrous things which help me develop a philosophy that strengthens my commitment to living, excites me and keeps me on purpose. This philosophy enables me to experience the joy of achievement, success and fulfillment in ways I may never have experienced without my health difficulties.

I am indeed a fortunate man. My life is unfolding as it should. I'm aware. I'm on purpose.

I encourage you also to increase your awareness and to get on purpose. No matter what your circumstance, no matter what the prognosis for your future, consider the concepts suggested in the pages of this book and use those that strengthen you and help you climb to the top of your own spirituality. From that lofty perch you will begin to experience the power and majesty of your own life. This will strengthen and energize you to press on to fulfill the dream God assigned to you when you were born . . . Let us press on, gallant pilgrim. Let us press on and on and on . . .

Your Death Is None of Your Business:
The Legend of the Wildflower

When the time of death approaches, be aware that we all hasten toward that time and place when we will make the same transition. Do not be afraid. You have made a similar transition before. It was at the time of your birth when you entered this world.

And do not put much weight on precise predictions of your time of release from this earthly passage. You are bound by no one's schedule, save God's. But if you have been provided with foreknowledge of the approaching departure, you have the advantage of a keener awareness that life is a passage. Because of this awareness, you, more than others, have time and opportunity to create a beautiful legacy that will endure beyond the time of your journey here.

Focus your energy and strength, not on the pain and dread of waiting, but on creating your legacy of courage and love. Act with purpose and fervor, for your activity will provide you with strength and resolve. Your example will also teach others the way of purposeful living.

Be careful that you do not retreat into self-pity. Self-pity fosters an attitude of ominous vulnerability and weakness. Those dark feelings foment anger which will find expression in unrealistic, selfish demands upon friends and family. There is no time for that. Your illness and your death are not the issue. More precisely, your death is not your business. Your death is God's business. But God charged you with the gift of life, so your business is your life and what you will do with it.

One of the great fears of dying is the fear that we will not be missed when we leave this terrestrial realm. Learn the lesson of the wildflower and put this fear to rest.

The wildflower flourishes and blooms. Living in beauty and splendor, it stays the allotted number of days. Near the end of its time, when spring rains cease and the heat of approaching summer dries the ground and leaves it parched, the wildflower loses luster. Petals wither, then droop, and the flower bows its head. Death is near, but before the final summons the dying plant exerts one last surge of strength. With a burst of energy it puts forth a blossom more beautiful and delicate than all the rest. The radiant blossom survives only a few precious hours. But before the wildflower withers in death, the blossom falls to the ground, scattering seeds, leaving a legacy of beauty that will endure and multiply for many seasons to come.

You, gallant pilgrim, have a similar opportunity. So gather your strength. Sow your love and beauty in example and service. Your deeds and inspiration will create a splendid legacy that will endure many generations.

And you, healthy pilgrims of strong body and hardy spirit, glory in your good fortune and the blessings of vigor and endurance. But take heed: Ancient writings teach us that we know not the time or the hour when the end shall come. You will be wise to learn the lesson of the wildflower. For it is better to sow love and beauty with many blossoms than to wait for the last.

Please God, when it's my time,
let death sneak up and catch me
hard at work
on a loving act of kindness.

Death is not the event
that ends your life.
For all intents and purposes,
your life ends
when you lose your dream.

It is not the diagnosis of your illness
that is most important.
It is your perception of the diagnosis
that makes the difference.
If you perceive the diagnosis to be the end,
that is what it will be.
If you perceive the diagnosis
to be an opportunity to live your life
in a new way,
then it will be so.

If you were not afraid of being born

into this world,

why fear being born into the next?

Those not involved in growth and life
are involved in withering and death.

Sorry, I Won't Have Time to Go to My Funeral

I'd like to go, I really would, but I won't have time. I have so many things yet to accomplish. Yes, I realize my body is dead. But, you see, my body is the only part of me that has expired. The most important part, the part that is me, my spirit, my soul, that part will never die. My spirit continues on, and my quest to fulfill the dream God assigned to me grows ever more intense. My way becomes more sure with each new step of the journey. I am filled with an exciting urgency. I am experiencing a great need to get on with it. For a truth that I had difficulty grasping while I was with you is now a truth I find abundantly clear. That truth: I was not a human being who sometimes had the spiritual experience; I am a spiritual being who had the human experience. That human experience, though fraught with difficulties and pain, was truly wonderful. It played a vital role in leading me toward fulfilling the dream God assigned to me at birth. The experience revealed many opportunities for me to raise my soul to higher service, love and awareness. I must hasten to capitalize on those opportunities.

I suppose, upon reflecting on my human experience, one might conclude that my life was exceedingly blemished, scarred with mistakes and fraught with sins. I was often lazy, weak and foolish. But I now know that those mistakes and sins are not permanent blemishes and scars. They are only editing marks to indicate places where I need to be more thoughtful, courageous, strong and diligent. Places where I need to expand and improve my spiritual performance. Those marks will eventually be erased as I grow and improve. That is why I cannot afford to take time to go to my funeral. I have so much to do that simply cannot wait.

You see, I must fulfill the dream God assigned to me. I can only do this if I am at my best spiritual self.

And neither should you spend much time or effort on the ceremony of my eulogy and good-bye. You, too, have much to do. Ancient writings instruct us to let the dead bury the dead. Let those who are dead in spirit attend to the rituals of funeral ceremony. God is God of the living, not the dead!

My spirit lives. I am with God.

Be with God also and be alive in spirit as I am alive. For God also assigned a dream to you when you were born. Your mission on earth is to discover that dream—to discover your purpose. When you have discovered your purpose, which is God's dream for you, work with all your might to accomplish it. Accomplish the work assigned to you and abide in love. Love yourself, your family, all of God's children and all of creation. For the greatest of all deeds and thought is love.

No, I will not be at my funeral. But please do not take my absence as an affront or an indication that I do not treasure you. Simply understand that I love you and I will continue to express my love in many ways, which will always make your life better and stronger if you open your heart and recognize my love. My spirit abides with you, and yours with me, until we can embrace and laugh together once again.

When you know and trust

the one walking beside you,

you need never fear again.

When I, in awesome wonder,
scan the night sky,
I find a tiny speck of light
near the constellation Pegasus.
That speck of light
is the Spiral Galaxy in Andromeda.
It is as large as our Milky Way,
and is but one of 100 million galaxies.
It has 100 billion suns,
each larger than our own sun.
When I think of all of this,
I can no longer believe in the God
my mother told me about,
nor can I believe in the God
I was taught to praise in Sunday school.
I'm compelled to believe in a God
immensely greater.

Death Is When We Put on a New Suit

I agree with those pundits who have said life is a journey aboard a beautiful spaceship called earth. But I further suggest that the purpose of this challenging human excursion is to enlighten and expand our spirits. Once enlightened, our spirits are ready to gain knowledge, wisdom and the skills necessary to continue on to the next higher plane.

While on board spaceship earth, which appears to

be a temporary duty station for the spirit, we are each fitted with a space suit. We commonly refer to these space suits as bodies. The suits are specially designed for this assignment and are crafted and equipped to gather, process and transmit important human data to our spirits for interpretation and storage for later use.

These disposable suits are notorious for design, material and structural flaws. They often require attention and maintenance. Tears and external repairs are usually quite simple. But when appendages such as hands or legs are torn off or badly damaged, they are quite often replaced with a manufactured facsimile. Internal parts, such as hearts, lungs and kidneys, also frequently become inoperable or critically damaged. When these parts cannot be repaired, they may be replaced with parts salvaged from suits that have been abandoned by spirits who have transitioned to new duty assignments.

Our space suits are made to last for the duration of this temporary duty assignment, and no longer. When the human mission is completed and it comes time to move on to a more challenging assignment, we crawl out of these disposable suits. They are left behind where some are harvested for spare parts, and then all are either buried or burned.

Although there is little evidence, and almost no solid information about future duty stations, it is likely that our spirits will be fitted into more sophisticated suits for the next mission at a new duty station.

How fascinating it is to think about what it will be like to explore our next spacecraft assignment in our brand-new suits when we are welcomed on board that flight.

On spaceship earth,

we are either casual passengers

occupying a seat

or working crew members

dedicated to the safety

and well-being of the ship

and all those on board.

I will not waste my life

looking for unanimity

and devising means.

Rather,

I will talk less,

plan less

and do more.

And miles to go before I sleep,

And miles to go before I sleep.

—Robert Frost

Blessed Are They . . .

Blessed are they who serve unselfishly, for they shall be esteemed and honored.

Blessed are they who join with others to accomplish goals and dreams, for they shall be rewarded with abiding love and friendship.

Blessed are they who understand that we are components of one another, for they shall be free of racism, bigotry and rejection.

Blessed are they who listen, for they shall be sought out and admired above all others.

Blessed are they who do not strive to dominate, for they shall win everlasting cooperation, warmth and companionship.

Blessed are they who do not use love and friendship for ulterior purposes, for they shall be cherished as valued companions.

Blessed are they who are sensitive to others, for they shall promote harmony, peace and love.

Blessed are they who do not look for perfection in others, for they shall be accepted and loved.

Blessed are they who see potential in others, for they shall be stimulating and attractive companions.

Blessed are they who settle differences as they arise, for they shall keep relationships free from mis-understandings.

Blessed are they who are open and truthful, for their relationships shall be warm, trusting and sincere.

Blessed are they who refuse to look for slights, for they shall feel loved and secure.

Blessed are they who are not petty, for they shall not be treated with pettiness.

Blessed are they who do not seek to do good, but simply strive to love and serve, for do-gooders are shunned and avoided, but a gracious, loving attitude is warmly received.

Blessed are they who help others help themselves, for they shall be loved and admired as wise mentors.

Blessed are they who keep cheerfulness and laughter as an integral part of their personality, for they shall be happy.

Blessed are they who strive to fulfill the dream God assigned to them when they were born, for they shall abound in joy and a successful and productive life.

Discover the Great
Purpose of Your Life

Do the work you love, for this is the only way to fulfill the dream that was assigned to you when you were born. Some may ask, What is the work I love? What is the dream that was assigned to me at birth?

The answer to these questions will continue to confound and frustrate you until you begin to understand the great purpose of your life. Yet, through the ages, the wisest of the wise have struggled to find the answer to the question "What is the purpose of life?" The answer has always been elusive, not because the question is difficult, but because it has been improperly asked. The question, as asked, suggests there is an answer suitable for all humankind. This is not the case. Each individual can be likened to the organs of the body. In the body, the heart has its own purpose, and so do the eyes and ears. If the ears attempt the work of the heart, or if the heart tries to function as the eyes, none of the organs fulfill the purpose for which they were intended. But if each organ fulfills the great purpose assigned to it at birth, the result is harmonious and the body functions beautifully. So it is with your life as an important part in the body of the universe.

The question, then, is not, "What is the purpose

of life?" but instead, "What is the purpose of *my* life?"

God intended that you discover the purpose of your life, but it is not an easy undertaking, because your purpose is concealed deep beneath layers of your unique gifts and talents. You must search through those layers, examine each gift and determine its function in your life. Diamonds and precious metals of the earth are mined in much the same way. And only those who possess strength, character and abiding commitment will persevere to search out and reap the blessings of the riches of diamonds and precious metals. So it is with the blessings and riches of a purposeful life. Through the process of meticulously uncovering your gifts and conscientiously using them to determine your course, your purpose will be revealed.

But proceed with patience and wisdom or you

may decide upon your purpose too quickly. Thoughtfully and carefully examine each of your gifts and talents, then determine how each applies to your life. It is God's plan that this be an arduous task, because in your struggle you will discover and come to understand great and wondrous truths about yourself. These truths are the keys to learning the great purpose of your life.

There once was a man who possessed the gifts of speech and communication. Aware of his gifts, he first used them for the purpose of selling goods. He became a powerful salesman. His reward was success and wealth. But that was not the dream God assigned to him at birth, and he was not happy. He then used his gifts for the purpose of politics. He was elected to high office. His reward was recognition, praise and glory. But neither was this the dream God assigned to him at birth, and he was not happy. He then used his gifts for the purpose of teaching little children. His reward was the joy and satisfaction of his work. He fulfilled the dream God had assigned to him at birth, and he was happy.

Use your gifts to discover the work you love so you can keep pace with the needs of your soul. To do work you despise brings anguish to the soul and takes you in a direction away from the majesty of your life.

Determining your special gifts and then using them for your great purpose is the abiding challenge of your life. This challenge must be taken lightly by no one. For the awareness and use of your special gifts is the source of your brilliance and enthusiasm. Awareness and the utility of those gifts brightens your countenance and improves your bearing and demeanor. It stimulates growth and knowledge, and becomes a source of inspiration to others.

When you come to know your gifts and use them for your great purpose, you become much like a fine musical instrument playing beautiful music every hour of the day. The greatest tragedy of life is to go to your grave with your music unplayed.

The alternative to using your gifts for a purposeful life is to endure work that does not hold the passions of your heart. Such work portrays you as dull and dispassionate. You are perceived as lethargic, unexciting and ordinary.

Do not be afraid to pursue the goals of your heart. But have great fear of toiling all your days in work that destroys your creativity and passion. Such work destroys the very essence of you. The most destructive fear is the fear that prevents you from letting go of a life that is destroying you.

The path of self-discovery and self-realization is the path that spirals upward to greatness. This is because your personal path to greatness is paved with nothing more than your own gifts and talents. Heed them. But be aware: The urge to greatness, though common, is seldom acted upon. Why is this so?

Ultimately, the character traits that impede the pursuit of a purposeful life of greatness are laziness and lethargy. Many become energized with the urge for greatness, but promptly lie down and wait to begin tomorrow. Laziness and lethargy destroy passions of the soul. Overcome laziness and lethargy and all other impediments will be overcome. If you do not overcome these flaws of character, you are destined to wallow in mediocrity and, eventually, in regret of a wasted life.

Be bold. A life of purpose requires boldness and courage. But the courageous life is the most exciting way to live. Far better to do the work you love, to live your purpose, than take rank with those poor souls who wallow in the desperate doldrums brought on by an unfulfilled life.

And do not despair if you have lacked the courage to launch your life on the journey of purpose and greatness. Courage is not something you lack. Courage is always an option. Choose this moment to act with courage and begin today to realize the dream God assigned to you when you were born.

The human race moves forward
with the achievements
of the outstanding individual.
You can be that individual.

Too many talented people
string and unstring their instruments
without ever playing their music.

Keep climbing upward.

You may not reach the top,

but the summit is definitely in that direction.

If you do not give

one hundred percent to achieving goals,

you will have too much extra time to worry about

why you aren't successful.

If you do not want to work hard enough

to succeed,

you will use any excuse

to fail.

You may be one of the truly great
people of our generation,
but we won't know for sure
until you prove it.

Are you taking your life

in a new direction,

or will it be more of the same?

Who Do You Think
You Are?

Who do you think you are, some kind of
conquering hero? Friends derisively
taunted the boy Napoleon as he pre-
tended he was a great military commander. The lad
drew detailed maps of the island of Corsica, prepared
battle plans and sketched overlays for troop place-
ments and defenses long before he ever set foot on a
battlefield . . .

Who do you think you are, a wealthy hotel owner? Acquaintances chided young Conrad Hilton, who imagined himself operating grand hotels long before he ever bought one . . .

Who do you think you are, the Great Alexander? Tutors teased the youthful prince who was later to become Alexander the Great. He pictured battles vividly in his mind long before he actually went onto battlefields to conquer all of the known world before he was thirty-five years old . . .

I think I am smart enough to learn, signed the deaf, mute and blind Helen Keller. She went on to overcome severe handicaps and conquer great difficulties to become one of the most celebrated women of all time . . .

As a person thinketh in his heart, so is he, proclaimed the wise King Solomon.

Who do you think you are?

You Are Your Greatest Asset. How Are You Managing It?

You are the most important person in your world. This is true because the way you conduct yourself controls the way you are valued by almost everyone around you. Thus, you are your most important asset. Manage this asset with the greatest of care, because it holds potential for enormous achievement and success.

Further, learn the secret for increasing your

greatest asset. Few before you have discovered it, even though the quest to uncover the secret has been the driving ambition of the great, and all those desiring greatness, since the beginning of time. Many claim to have found it. Some say the secret for increasing your greatest asset is riches, fame, approbation, power or the accumulation of some other psychological or material gain. Others claim the secret is hidden beneath a complex puzzle of personal and sociological forces which interact to predetermine behavior and nullify personal responsibility. These people say the secret can only be discovered by mind doctors and social healers—those who redefine mores and values.

Yet the secret for increasing your greatest asset is incredibly simple. The secret: Appreciate other people more.

Practice treating others with value and respect.

You will be amazed at how quickly you will become the most cherished, valued, respected and successful person you know, and the value of your greatest asset will soar.

The fears that keep you

from venturing out

are the fears

that keep you alone.

If you have no friends
and no place to go,
it is up to you
to do something about it—
it is your responsibility.

If others do not like you
when you're being yourself,
there is little you should do
to change their minds.

The ultimate waste of life

is to spend it

trying to adapt to people and things

you don't even like.

The Secret of the Purpose
and Meaning of Life

A young attorney rushing through the courthouse park came upon an old man humming contentedly to himself as he carved the form of a bird from a block of wood. The carver was so serenely intent on the detail of his work that the lawyer paused to watch. He lingered to peruse several delightful wood sculptures on display next to the craftsman. Finally, the attorney asked, "What is this you're doing? Are you selling these?"

The old man looked up from his work and smiled, noticing the attorney for the first time. "I'm returning my gift," he replied pleasantly, "and no, I am not selling them, I'm giving them away. Would you like to have one?" Without waiting for a reply, he turned again to his carving.

The attorney, immediately suspicious of the offer of a free gift, asked, "What do you mean you're returning your gift? Why are you giving these things away?"

The old man set his work aside carefully and studied the questioner. "Do you know the secret?" he asked respectfully.

"You didn't answer my question," the attorney replied. "And what secret are you talking about?"

"Come, sit with me," the old man invited warmly,

smiling. "I sense you could use a moment of quiet contemplation. I will tell you the secret."

The old craftsman spoke with a soft accent. There was a peaceful knowing confidence about him. In spite of himself, the attorney was attracted to the old man. He studied his watch before stiffly taking a seat on the bench. "I have a little time before my next appointment." There was a patronizing expression on his face. "Hurry and tell me your story."

The old man smiled patiently. "Of course," he said. "It will take only a moment to tell you the secret—the secret of the purpose and meaning of life. The secret was told to me by my father, who learned it from his father, who . . ."

"Yes, yes," the attorney prodded. "Please get on with your story."

"The secret," the old man declared, "is that the purpose of your life is to discover the special gift God has concealed deep within you." The attorney smiled derisively at the mention of God. The carver went on.

"To fulfill your purpose, you must search diligently to discover your gift—a gift that is not easily found. And it is well hidden for a very good reason." He measured his words and squinted his eyes for emphasis. "You see, God knows that in your diligent search you will learn many wondrous and powerful things about yourself . . . things you would never learn unless you are looking for your concealed gift.

"But be careful," the old man admonished. "You will likely come across several gifts and talents that a clever man such as yourself is capable of doing pretty well. The things you do pretty well do not qualify as your special gift. Your special gift is a talent you do so well that few, if any, can match your skill in performing it." The old wood-carver studied his listener. He had the attorney's full attention.

"The search will become exasperating. At times you will be tempted to cease your quest and choose a gift for the sake of expediency. But do not use expediency as the reason for choosing," the old man cautioned. "For only the discovery and development of your *special* gift will provide you with true happiness, fulfillment and greatness.

"There will likely be other times," the carver suggested, "when you will be tempted to reject a particular gift because it seems to lack potential to provide you with adequate income or material wealth. Beware of rejecting a gift for that reason. We are told," he said, gesturing widely with both hands, "that we do not know the mind of God. We must be careful not to impose our simple logic, machinations and desires over the plans of God. God has promised that if we are truly committed to doing the work for which He has prepared us, our heart's desires will be provided. That is God's solemn promise," the carver avowed fervently. "But until you discover your unique gift, declare it and then use it with all the strength of your mind and body, you will ricochet through life never finding a place of peace, contentment and success."

The young attorney was totally captivated by the wise old carver's words. He urged him to continue. "I understand the importance of finding one's purpose," he said, "but you also mentioned the meaning of life. Where does that come in?"

"Ah, yes, the meaning of life. The meaning of your life will be revealed to you as you develop your gift, use it to provide for yourself and those you love, and then give it away."

"Give it away?" the attorney challenged.

"Yes. Give it away." The sculptor paused. "You

see, God gave you the gift so that you can provide yourself with a good and abundant life. In return, He asks that you express thanks for the gift by giving it to others. Giving is an expression of love. In His infinite wisdom, God knows that your gift of love will be returned to you generously, and often in mysterious ways, so that your life will take on glorious meaning."

The attorney settled himself more comfortably next to the old man and quietly considered all he had heard. Finally, he spoke. "By being here in the park, carving your birds and then giving them away, you are bringing meaning to your life?"

"You are partly right," said the old man. "But my special gift is not carving birds. Carving is just a gift I do pretty well. My special gift is that of an awakener."

"An awakener?"

"Yes, I was fortunate. I discovered early in my life

that I have a unique talent and ability to awaken people to the great possibilities in their lives. For many years I earned a satisfying and comfortable living awakening young minds as a teacher in the classroom." Wistfully, the old man smiled, recalling many pleasant and stimulating years as an educator. "Slumbering in the deep recesses of young minds," he went on, "are profound thoughts, insights and ideas awaiting the nudge of a skilled awakener. I took great delight in that awakening." Pride radiated from his pleased expression. "I was a great teacher," he almost whispered. "I give thanks every day for that gift.

"But forgive my meanderings. You asked if carving birds brought meaning to my life. The answer is yes, but that is not the reason I carve our beautiful winged friends. I carve them as a means of attracting people such as yourself to come sit and talk with me. This provides me with the opportunity to give my special gift away. As I talk with people and awaken them to the great possibilities slumbering within, I give them my gift.

"Now," the carver said, smiling broadly, "let us talk about your special gift and whether or not you have found the meaning in your life."

The two, now fast friends, talked on and on, speaking of wondrous gifts and discussing ways they could best use them and give them away.

If either the possession
or the lack of worldly goods
and riches
gives you no contentment,
you have not yet found
your life's work.

Just being an encouragement
to someone who is discouraged
can make you feel successful.

It's always exciting
to discover new talent,
but the most exciting
place to discover it
is in yourself.

Loneliness Can Be
a Self-Inflicted Wound

There once was a man who trudged daily to his place of work. He performed his work adequately and earned his pay. He was not well known. He was seldom even noticed by those in his workplace. Day after day, life was dreary. His heart was heavy, for he felt insignificant, sad and lonely.

The man's loneliness and discontent filled his

soul. He grew increasingly bitter. He vowed he would inflict loneliness on his fellow workers just as they had inflicted it upon him, not knowing this would deepen the wounds of loneliness within himself. He decided that he would extend no courtesies in the workplace, nor would his smile bless those with whom he worked.

He continued in this manner and his heart remained sad and lonely. One night during troubled sleep, a vision came to him in a dream. He saw himself sitting in front of a stove shivering from cold because there was no fire in the stove. Both he and the stove were very cold. In the dream he cursed the stove. "Give me warmth and I will give you wood," he ordered. The stove paid no heed. There was no warmth, only bitter cold. The man cursed the stove again, shouting, "Why do you provoke me so, leaving me cold and shivering?"

In the morning he awoke unrested and ill-tempered.

On the next night and the next, and for many nights thereafter, the same vision appeared in the man's dreams. He continued to curse the stove. He became more and more angry.

One night the man shivered with such bitter cold that he feared he would freeze to death, so real was his dream. In fear and desperation he ran out into the forest shouting back at the stove, "You are a pathetic, evil thing! You could give me warmth, but you selfishly refuse. I will pile wood into your belly and light it to warm myself. I will not allow you to cause my death!" Upon returning from the forest, he loaded wood into the stove and lit it. A crackling fire soon warmed him. He went again to the forest and returned with more wood, heaping it into the stove.

The stove now glowed with heat from the fire. The man and the entire house were warmed. He continued to supply wood, and the stove provided abundant warmth.

The next morning he awoke rested and in good humor. He whistled as he walked to work. He smiled at strangers along the way. They waved to him and wished him a good day. He entered the workplace with a happy, glowing heart. He greeted fellow workers and asked about their well-being and inquired about their families. Fellow workers responded cheerily and added how glad they were to see him.

The man no longer felt angry or lonely. He became aware that by withdrawing and being rude to others he had inflicted loneliness on himself. The stove in his dream had taught him he could not get warmth unless he was first willing to provide the wood. The man had learned the lesson of friendship. No one can expect acceptance unless he is first willing to give of himself.

When you define your life

in terms of burdens, hurts, fears

and oppressing obligations,

you give the perfect definition of failure.

We are all acting out of love,

or out of the need for love.

If you don't think it's a good day,

just try missing one.

If you focus on your pains and scars,

others will too.

Thinking in terms

of your problems

empowers those problems

to hold you in their grip.

Think in terms

of solutions

and you will be set free.

When problems become bigger
than your desire for accomplishment,
you start sliding backward.

You will always
make your fears
as big as they need to be
to keep from doing
what you don't want to do.

Much of the intrigue

and mischief

we suspect in others

is aroused by what

we know of ourselves.

Redemption of a Bag Lady

A beautiful little girl played busily and contentedly all the day long. When she felt love, she sang and snuggled with those she loved. When she was happy, her laughter tinkled merrily, and when she was sad, she cried. When she felt anger, she scolded. When she was tired, she lay down to sleep, and when she awoke, she skipped and jumped with the joy of life. Her days were filled with curiosity and wonderful adventures. She ran happily through childhood, for she had no baggage to carry.

As she grew older, she accepted responsibilities and responded to the needs of others. But still she loved and sang with those she loved, and her laughter tinkled merrily. She cried when she was sad, and she expressed anger when she was offended. And when she was tired, she lay down to sleep. When she awoke, she skipped and jumped with the joy of life. But she was now carrying a small, decorated bag, in which she placed the disappointments and pains of life.

As she grew and matured, a new kind of beauty graced her appearance. Her bearing was assured and confident. She ventured into the world and experienced new awarenesses. Still she loved and sang with those she loved, her laughter tinkled merrily, she cried when she was sad, expressed anger when she was offended, and when she was tired, she lay down to sleep. But when she awoke, she seldom skipped and jumped with the joy of life, for the bag in which she placed ever more pains, disappointments, resentments and angers was becoming heavy.

She became a woman of the world, with friends and admirers, busy with her career and bright future. Her youthful trust was replaced with wariness and sophistication. Still she loved and sang with those she loved, her laughter tinkled merrily, she cried when she was sad, and she expressed anger when she was offended. But she had difficulty sleeping, and when she awoke, she no longer skipped and jumped with the joy of life. The bag she carried was rapidly filling. It was cumbersome, and tending it occupied much of her time.

She married the man of her dreams. Together they planned their family and life together. She loved and sang with those she loved, her laughter tinkled merrily, and she cried when she was sad. But she no longer expressed anger when she was offended. She had difficulty sleeping, and when she awoke, she could no longer skip and jump with the joy of life. The bag she carried was tattered and filled to overflowing. She went cautiously lest the contents spill out and embarrass her.

She became a mother, and her children were healthy, happy and beautiful. She was busy making a home, working and serving her community. She loved and sang with those she loved, and her laughter tinkled merrily, but she no longer cried when she was sad and no longer expressed anger when she was offended. Her sleep was restless and troubled, and when she awoke, she no longer skipped and jumped with the joy of life. The bag containing the pains, disappointments, resentments and angers of her life would hold no more. She began searching for a better way to carry her bag, for she felt that she needed it with her at all times.

Her children grew in stature and in knowledge and began families of their own. Her offspring were a tribute to her. But she felt lonely and abandoned. Still she loved and sang with those she loved, but her laughter no longer tinkled merrily, she no longer cried when she was sad and she no longer expressed anger when she was offended. She barely slept, and when she awoke, she was too tired to skip and jump with the joy of life. She found an abandoned shopping cart and into it she dumped all the contents of the tattered bag containing the pains, disappointments, resentments and angers of her life. Now she had room for even more pain, resentment, disappointment and anger. She doggedly pushed the cart with her everywhere she went.

Outwardly, she was a handsome, mature woman, admired for her graciousness. But she felt her youth leaving her. Still she loved, but no longer sang with those she loved. Her laughter no longer tinkled merrily, she no longer cried when she was sad and no longer expressed anger when she was offended. She paced the floor at night. Her time and strength were used to gather more pain, resentment, disappointment and anger for her cart. The cart was heavily laden, filled to overflowing. It was nearly impossible to push. But she struggled to push it with her at all times.

One day, although worn, tired, filled with anger and reluctant to abandon her cart for even a moment, she agreed to care for her grandchild. To her surprise, in the presence of the beautiful child, she found herself smiling, her heart swelling with love as she and the child played contentedly all the day long.

Marveling at the fresh exuberance of the child, she set her cart aside. With great joy she experienced a glorious redemption.

When the child felt love, she and the grandmother sang and snuggled. When the child was happy, her laughter tinkled merrily and the grandmother laughed with her, and when the child was sad, she cried and the grandmother cried. When the child felt anger, she expressed it and the grandmother also scolded, and when the child was tired, she and the grandmother lay down to sleep. When they awoke, they skipped and jumped with the joy of life.

. . . unless you change and become as
little children you shall not enter
the kingdom . . .
—Matthew 18:3

When people talk incessantly
about problems and pains,
there's something about them
that serves a purpose
in their lives.

In even the most

damaged lives

there are vast

undamaged areas.

If you're still living

with the pain and resentment

of your youth,

maybe it's time to grow up.

Do you ever wonder
how God could do this to you
after all you've done for Him?

Science-Theology:
Two Faces of the Same God

Two esteemed professionals, both leaders in their respective fields, gazed reverently upon an ugly brown biological mass on the table in front of them. One was a scientist, the other a theologian. In respectful wonder they contemplated the small, amorphous lump. Locked within the layers and folds of the mysterious object was the evidential basis for their conflicting philosophies and beliefs on the secret of life. Each had come to try to convince the other, and the assembled audience of partisan disciples, of the validity and legitimacy of his or her personal faith and doctrine.

The scientist was first to step forward. Gingerly, she picked up the brown thing, which she identified as a common tulip bulb. "Contained within this small tulip bulb," she said, "is the complex secret of life which will one day burst forth as a beautiful flower. But rather than resort to superstition, theological mumbo jumbo or guesswork for understanding the reasons this will occur, I will unravel the secret by using scientific fact, knowledge and logic."

The scientist proceeded to explain the sophisticated structure of plant cells, offering empirical evidence for the role and function of such phenomena as plastids, homeostasis and photosynthesis. She presented a scholarly description of the DNA molecule within the tulip bulb that contained a miniscule imprint—a tiny picture in minute detail of the flower that was to be. The scientist quoted from impressive scientific manuscripts and referred to respected journals to support and enhance her convincing argument. "It is the opinion of the greatest scientific minds," she said, winding down her impressive performance, "that when all of these events occur and come together within this tulip bulb, the spark of life will be ignited and we will have the eventual emergence of a beautiful blossom."

The theologian stepped forward to take his turn. He accepted the tulip bulb from the scientist. He held the small bulb at arm's length and studied it carefully. Finally, he began to speak. "My learned friend has made a persuasive argument," he said. "But I hasten to add, she has neglected to address one important aspect. My friend did not speak of the force, the energy, the love, that causes all of the things she so carefully described to come together. For it cannot be explained without reference to the divine power that brings all of the phenomena together at precisely the right time. What is this power? Show it to me!"

The theologian leveled a challenging stare at his opponent. The scientist met his gaze and smiled confidently. The ecclesiastic turned resolutely back to his argument. "My friend will never be able to explain it or show it to us," he continued. "She has aptly described the command center of this little tulip bulb, but she neglected to describe the commander. If you were to take this tulip bulb and dissect it into paper-thin slices, and then magnify those slices two thousand times, you would still find no evidence of the force that brought it all together. But the divine power is there . . . We know it's there. Our knowing is called faith. Faith that one day soon God will cause everything to happen just as He planned, and a beautiful flower will emerge from this ugly lump." He proceeded to reference passages of Holy Scripture, then paused dramatically to examine the faces of those around him.

Suddenly, a voice as of a rushing mighty wind resounded from above. *"Oh ye of small minds!"* the voice cried. *"Do you not know that your foolish dispute is not about whether there is a God. The reason for your disagreement is the pointless labeling and naming of your individual god. One speaks of the evidential proof of the creative intelligence of the god of science. The other speaks of manifestations of the god of spirit. Hear my words! You speak of separate aspects of the same God. Each of you has a purpose. Go, and be filled with the wonder and majesty of all things of the universe according to your purpose."*

A hush descended upon the room. The scientist,

heeding the voice from above, rushed to worship and sing praises in her cathedral. Her cathedral was filled with test tubes, beakers, centrifuges, microscopes and gleaming scientific machines. The liturgy of her worship was drawn from the words of profound scientific textbooks, journals, and manuscripts of scientific experiment.

The theologian also heeded the voice and rushed to his cathedral to worship. His cathedral was furnished with eucharistic chalices, sacramental wines, altars, holy statues and icons of spiritual tribute. The liturgy for his worship was drawn from ancient scrolls, scriptures, and hymnals.

Thus, the two professionals, each with a different purpose and each in his and her own way, fulfilled their unique opportunity for service. Both became engaged in their own productive work, and there was no longer time for debate or argument.

Is there a chasm separating

God from humankind,

or is God within us,

just waiting for us to recognize Him?

Let us not quibble over what we call
the supreme organizing intelligence
which flows in and through
everything in the universe.
We can call it Universal Order;
we can call it Spirit;
we can call it Consciousness;
we can call it Soul;
we can call it Love;
we can call it Yahweh;
we can call it Allah;
we can call it Sophia,
or we can call it God.
It does not matter what we call it.
It is the great intelligence
that allows seedlings to sprout,
flowers to open every morning,
planets to hold their orbits,
the cosmos to maintain its place
and galaxies to be as they are.
We are all part of it.
We are all one.

Our Heroic Journeys

You do not remember your first heroic journey. It began when you were a microscopic creature wriggling in the depths of murky amniotic fluid in your mother's womb. You were eventually pushed out into a strange, dry, hostile environment. You learned to breathe air, to crawl, and then to stand erect and walk in magnificent splendor as a beautiful human being. What a heroic journey!

But that heroic journey, although remarkable, was only a precursor of an even more heroic journey yet to come . . . yet to come, that is, for those who are awakened to the great purpose of their lives.

Awakenings that lead to heroic journeys take many forms and come about in various ways. Some are hardly noticed, and others make lasting impacts on the world scene. Saul of Tarsus, who was to become the apostle Paul, is one dramatic example. He was traveling the road to Damascus on a sinister mission to find and persecute Christians when he was struck to the ground and blinded by a flashing light. Before his awakening, this man had breathed out threats and murder against the disciples of Christ. But after his awakening and conversion, his heroic journey led him to become the most influential person to ever preach the gospel of Jesus.

From This High Place

Most who undertake heroic journeys experience
awakenings far less dramatic than that of the apostle
Paul. My own awakening occurred in the weeks following a severe heart attack when I learned I faced
the likely prospect of an early death. This "brush
with death" evoked a strong welling up from within
that life was still expecting something important
from me. I recalled the words of Nietzsche: "He
who has the why to live, can bear most any how."
Discovering and fulfilling the expectations life held
for me became my "why" to live.

Surprisingly, the search and discovery was neither a long nor a difficult task. The simple method I
used may also help you in your quest to discover the
great purpose of your life.

The path that eventually led to discovering the
great purpose of my life started with my long-held
conviction that it is through the work we love that

we find the way to fulfill the dream that was assigned to us when we were born. My problem was that I did not know, with any certainty, what work I loved best. There were many things I liked to do, but I had no idea which one held the secret of the great purpose of my life.

But suddenly, almost miraculously, I realized what I needed to do to learn the great purpose for the rest of my life. I take no credit for this idea, because it came to me as a gift—a gift that I pass freely on to those who believe, as I do, that God assigns a dream to each of us when we are born. This simple procedure may also lead you to learn many powerful and wondrous things about yourself which will help point the way to the great purpose of your life.

To Learn the Great Purpose of Your Life

- Begin *today* to keep a journal.
- Make only one kind of entry in your journal. Simply describe the one thing you did during the day that you loved doing more than any other. Be sure to consider the things you do in work, in play and leisure (hobbies and leisure-time activities hold important clues) and in service. Do not describe your dreams and hopes. Describe only the things you actually do. There may be some days in which there is very little you loved doing. Even so, there will be at least one thing that you liked best. It is important that you record even that one thing, because it holds significant clues.
- Write your journal entry at the end of each day. Do not be concerned that you will forget some

event you loved doing if you do not write it down immediately. If you forget, it probably isn't all that important.

- Write each entry on a separate page.
- Be brief. You will seldom need more than three or four sentences. Do not go into the whys and wherefores of what you loved doing. Simply write a brief description so that you can recall the event later.
- Make entries every day of the week. Don't skip weekends.
- Do not go back to read previous entries. Rereading will unduly influence new entries. And do not write an ongoing story. Your intent should be to simply record the particular event you loved doing most on the day of the journal entry.
- Keep your journal for eight weeks.

• At the end of eight weeks take an uninterrupted block of time to read your journal through.

• Carefully divide all your journal entries into appropriate categories. For example, my categories, in no particular order, were:

teaching

writing

public speaking

reading and studying

being an encourager

designing and building

gardening

diet and exercise

family functions

social events

The categories from your journal will be uniquely yours. But it is important that you combine similar events into appropriate general categories.

• Determine which category has the most entries. There will likely be one category that has several times more entries than the others. Study this category and look carefully for clues that point you in a specific direction or toward a particular activity. These clues will lead you on the path toward discovery of the work you love. As you look for clues and gather evidence, always keep in mind that it is in the work you love that you will discover the great purpose of your life.

The category with the most entries in my journal—more than all the others put together—was being an "encourager." Under this category I had listed all the times I talked with friends, acquaintances, students and clients about ways to enjoy a more productive, meaningful life. I found that most of the people I talked to went away encouraged to work harder and to get their lives on purpose. The fact that I had been an encouragement to them was also a major source of inspiration for me.

I painstakingly studied and reflected on every entry in the category. Then I thought about the entire list as a group to see if they all fit into a general pattern. They did. The list helped me realize that I enjoyed—no, I *loved*—encouraging and counseling the people I cared about to find the great purpose of their lives. I also became acutely aware that many people sought me out looking for this counseling.

I then went to the library and began reading a carefully selected list of books and articles aimed toward expanding my knowledge of personal communication and counseling techniques. I found that I already possessed many of the talents and skills I needed to begin my heroic journey of encourager. This discovery led me to conclude that, at some level, I already knew the great purpose of my life. I had, in fact, already unknowingly begun my heroic journey. I have never been quite sure exactly when it began, but I suspect it occurred with my increasing awareness that I am not likely to enjoy a long life. But this new calculated evidence that resulted from keeping and studying my journal made me feel vibrant and alive. There was more purpose and direction in my life than I had ever experienced before. That purpose: to encourage fellow travelers on spaceship earth to dedicate themselves to finding the great purpose of their lives.

But contrary to what one might expect, the new awareness did not cause me to drastically alter my day-to-day activities. I did not change careers or suddenly go back to school. I simply intensified the role of encourager in everything I did. I practiced making *encouraging* an integral part of my personality.

As I pressed forward in my journey, joy, happiness, fulfillment and success came to me in ways I had never experienced before. I am quite sure my increased energy, focus and enthusiasm helped me earn many material things such as money and possessions, but they were of secondary importance compared to the richness of knowing I was fulfilling the dream God assigned to me when I was born.

But eventually, more serious health problems returned. I was forced to alter plans and goals. Since I first used my journal, health difficulties have caused me to make three major career changes. Each change, although initially stressful and disruptive, has led to exciting and fulfilling work. I sense that each change of direction has helped me to stay on purpose and to travel further along my heroic journey.

I am now on what I call the fourth leg of my journey. On this leg, my physical activity has of necessity been curtailed. As a result, I now use the written word combined with much shorter lectures and workshops as a means to encourage others to discover the dream that was assigned to them when they were born. I have little doubt this phase will be even more exciting and fulfilling than all the rest. But regardless, my entire journey to this point has thrilled and enthralled me.

Health problems continue. I have no doubt that my body is still trying to kill me. In spite of this, in a real sense, I count myself fortunate. I am keenly aware of my life-threatening gene—my insidious computer chip, and I stay alert for signs of attack. When I see signs, my doctors and I move quickly to stave off the attack. One doctor told me, "We're in a life-and-death chess match with your LP(a) gene. But if we keep our wits about us, I feel confident you will be able to *live* all the days of your life." For this I am extremely grateful.

The first step to greatness

is learning what we were meant to do.

It is only through

daring to explore

and extend ourselves

that we truly come alive.

Epilogue

There is one thing that we all share. We are all going to die. We may improve our quality of life, and we can postpone death for a day or a week or maybe even for a few years, but nothing will prevent our eventual exit from this life.

Consider this story: Long ago, a rich Persian prince was walking in his gardens. A servant rushed up to him, trembling. "I have just met Death," he wailed, "and Death looked down upon me and threatened me." The servant begged the master to give him his swiftest stallion so he could flee to Teheran, which he could reach on a fast horse that same evening. The prince granted the terrified servant's wish, and he galloped off.

Upon returning to his palace the prince himself met Death. "Why did you threaten and terrify my servant?" he demanded.

"I did not threaten your servant," said Death. "I only showed surprise in finding him here. I planned to meet him tonight in Teheran."

Death is a reality, and it is surely ahead for all of us. But the foolish servant in the story made the sad mistake of letting the fear and dread of death take control of his life.

Do not become like the servant. It will serve no

worthwhile purpose. Instead, focus on life and the useful things you are going to do with the rest of your life, and death will fade into insignificance. Furthermore, love, commitment and service quite often extend the days of our lives.

Events of my own life bear strong testimony to these facts. When I made a total commitment to the positive aspects of my journey, my role and reputation as an encourager grew and spread. I began speaking to various groups in my hometown, then I began speaking throughout California, then the entire United States, and eventually into Canada. My wife and valued business partner, Emma, and I have been far too busy to spend much time wallowing in depressing thoughts of my death. While we are occasionally discouraged and once in a while we contemplate our tenuous future, the abiding attitude that gives us strength and courage is this: If death wants us, it will have to rudely interrupt our busy schedule, because we simply do not have time to sit and wait for it.

Of course, we both know that death will eventually come to both of us. But in the meantime we are having the time of our lives.

Between speaking engagements I found time to write, and Emma found time to publish my thoughts and concepts. The first edition of this book was self-published under the title *Your Death Is None of Your Business*. Shortly after the book got into circulation, we began receiving letters from across the United States and Canada and from such distant places as Egypt and Australia. Readers wrote to comment on the encouragement and inspiration they received from the book.

One reader, whose son had recently died of AIDS, drove several hundred miles to give me the warmest embrace I have ever received. Through tears of gratitude, she said, "After the terrible diagnosis, my son's life was filled with fear, bitterness and self-pity. Then he read and understood the message of your book. Thank God, the last six weeks of his life were filled with a commitment to leave his beautiful legacy of strength, love and service. He died peacefully, leaving me with precious memories."

On another occasion, a man knocked on our door and introduced himself as Dr. Vincent Pratt from Vancouver, British Columbia. He had read the book. He was on vacation in California and had driven to Fresno to talk with me. He explained that he was involved in some revolutionary new work that had to do with restoring the immune system. My ears immediately perked up because my own doctors had told me my latest bouts with cancer had likely resulted from a deficient immune system. Emma and I eagerly talked with Dr. Pratt for most of the day. Before he left, he put me in touch with a colleague in California who is familiar with the work he is doing. Consequently, I am undergoing treatments that might possibly result in neutralizing my LP(a) gene. Had we not been out and about, speaking and writing, this could not have happened.

These incidents, and many others, reinforce my belief that a life of dedication and service is far superior to a life of desperate survival where fear determines most every activity.

There is so much important work to do. It makes no difference what your talents might be. Your station, condition or prognosis is not important. A heroic journey has nothing to do with intellect, ancestry or environment . . . it has everything to do with attitude, fortitude, character and commitment.

Act with courage now, for courage is always an

option. But a word of caution is in order. Scripture says this path of courage is narrow and few will find it. Yet I urge you to put forth a mighty effort to find the path, for those who do find it will dwell in this high place.

This is the true joy in life,

the being used for a purpose

recognized by yourself as a mighty one;

the being thoroughly worn out

before you are thrown on the scrap heap.

—GEORGE BERNARD SHAW

May you continue

to climb

toward your high place.